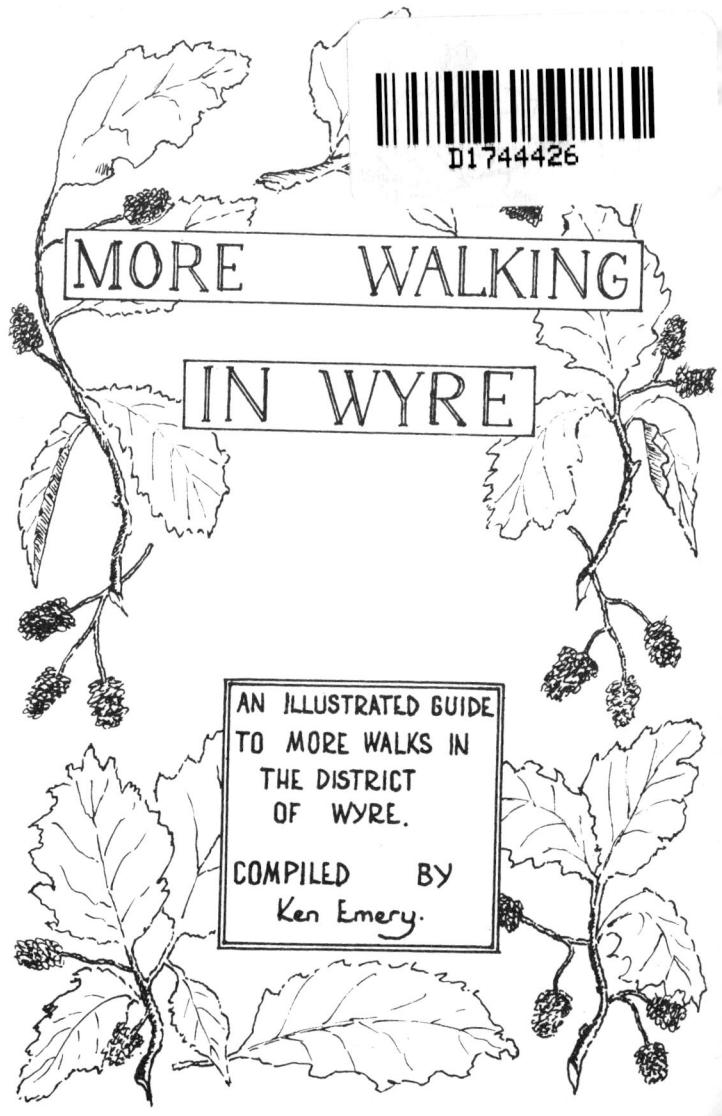

MORE WALKING

IN WYRE

AN ILLUSTRATED GUIDE
TO MORE WALKS IN
THE DISTRICT
OF WYRE.

COMPILED BY
Ken Emery.

More Walking in Wyre
by Ken Emery

First edition, April 1992
Published by Carnegie Publishing Ltd., 18 Maynard
Street, Ashton,Preston, PR2 2AL.

Text, maps and drawings by Ken Emery

Copyright © Ken Emery, 1992

All rights reserved
No part of this publication may be reproduced,
stored in a retrieval system, or transmitted in any
form or by any means, without the prior permission
of the publisher

ISBN 0 948789 88 3

Publishers' Notes

The Publishers (Carnegie Publishing Ltd) recommend that all walks are undertaken with reference to the relevant Ordnance Survey Pathfinder map.

All walkers are asked to observe the Country Code (see page ii) and not to stray onto private land where access is not indicated in the walk instructions.

Any comments with regard to walk instructions or any other part of the text should be addressed to the author and copyright holder, Ken Emery, care of the Publishers.

INTRODUCTION.

Following the publication of my first guide book, "Walking in Wyre," I received many encouraging comments from its readers and it is because of this encouragement that I have written this sequel "More Walking in Wyre".

Again I have kept to what has proved to be a successful formula which is to keep the book pocket-sized and to assume that the reader has the use of a motor-car. As before I have added historical notes which I hope give the walks additional interest. This time the walks vary from sedate Sunday afternoon strolls to a fairly strenuous fellwalk of seven and a half miles.

Once again sensible clothing and footwear is strongly advised to be worn on these walks. The Ordnance Survey Landranger Map No 102 or the Pathfinder series maps are useful in assisting navigation and can be used to modify these walks should you so wish.

Enjoy Wyre's beautiful countryside and please honour the Country Code.

Good walking!

Ken Emery 1991.

i

THE COUNTRY CODE.

Enjoy the countryside and respect its life and work.

Guard against all risk of fire.

Fasten all gates.

Keep your dogs under close control.

Keep to public paths across farmland.

Use gates and stiles to cross fences, hedges and walls.

Leave livestock, crops and machinery alone.

Take your litter home.

Help to keep all water clean.

Protect wild-life, plants and trees.

Take special care on country roads.

Make no unnecessary noise.

ACKNOWLEDGEMENTS.

I acknowledge the help given to me by I.C.I Hillhouse International and Mr. Ron Melling of Pilling for information and old photographs of the saltmine and brine production at Preesall. Thanks also to the Tourism and Countryside Section of the Wyre Borough Council for information and advice so readily given.

BIBLIOGRAPHY.

Historic Walks around Bleasdale.	John Dixon and Jaana Järvinen.
A History of Pilling.	F. J. Sobee.
More Windmill Land.	Allen Clarke.
An Album of Thornton - Cleveleys.	Catherine Rothwell.
Poulton-le-Fylde in times past.	— do —
Garstang and Fylde Album.	Albert Clayton.
The History of the Fylde.	John Porter.
The History of Blackpool.	William Thornber.
Skippool, old port of Poulton.	Graham Evans.
Excursions into Fylde History.	David Foster.
Place Names of Lancashire.	David Mills.
Fylde Regional Report.	Mawson.

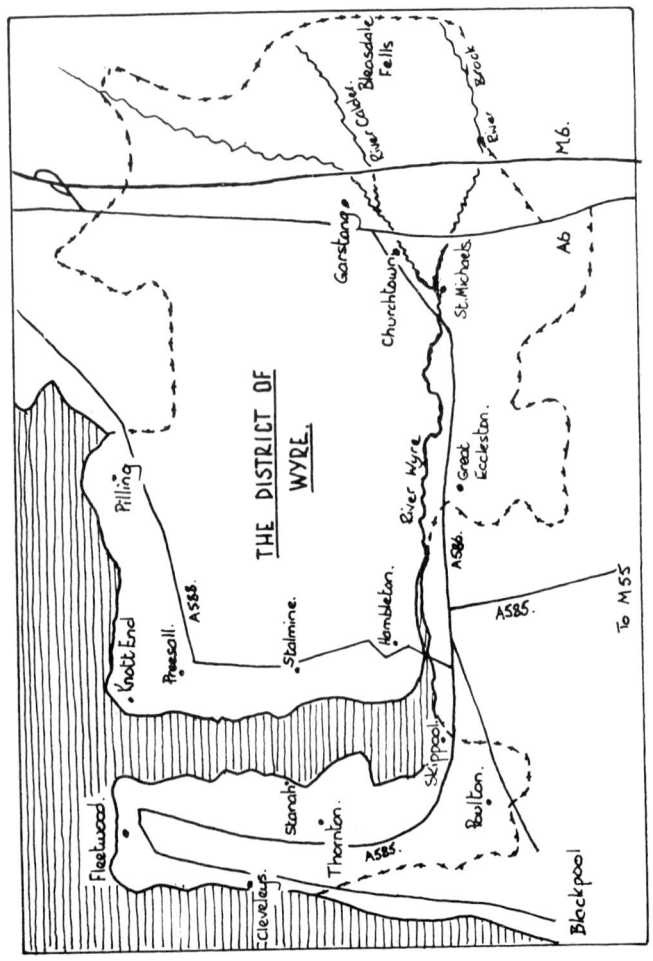

THE DISTRICT OF WYRE

CONTENTS.

Page.

BLEASDALE FELLS. A CIRCULAR WALK. .... 1.

A RIVERSIDE STROLL AT ST. MICHAELS. .... 17.

A WALK TO LADY HAMILTON'S WELL. .... 29.

A WALK IN AND AROUND THE VILLAGE OF
PILLING. .... 41.

SKIPPOOL AND LITTLE POULTON CIRCULAR
WALK. .... 55.

A WALK IN AND AROUND GREAT ECCLESTON. ...... 68.

A WALK IN AND AROUND THE VILLAGE OF
CHURCHTOWN. .... 78.

A WALK IN BLEASDALE. .... 91.

A WALK THROUGH THE SALT WORKINGS
OF PREESALL. .... 104.

BLEASDALE FELLS. A CIRCULAR WALK.

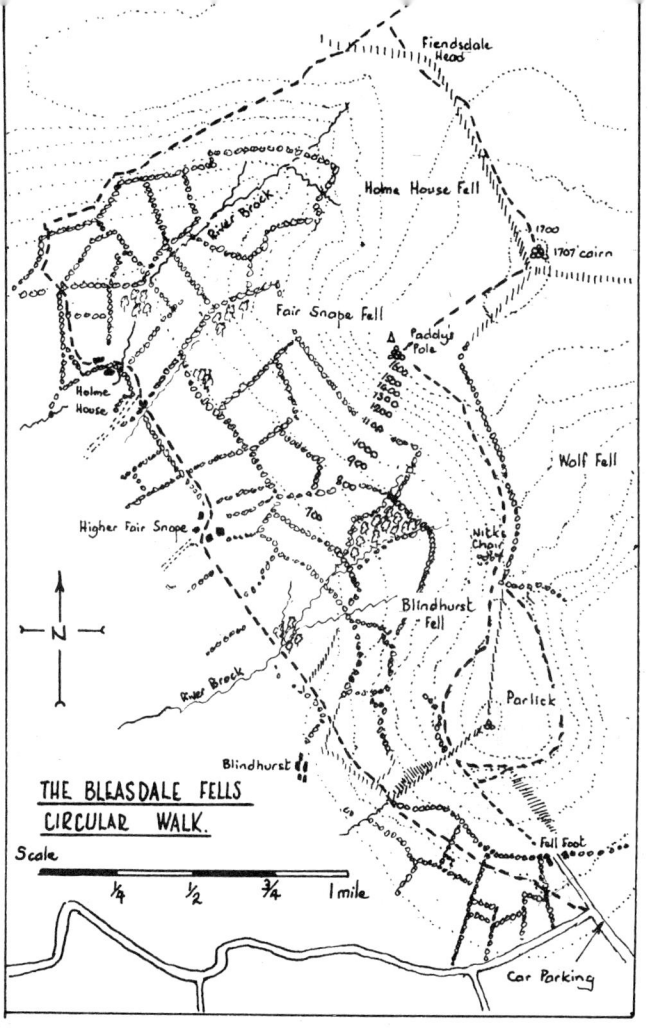

Fiendsdale Head

Holme House Fell

1700
1707' cairn

River Brock

Fair Snape Fell

△ Paddy's Pole

1500
1400
1300
1200

Holme House

1100

Wolf Fell

1000

900

Higher Fair Snope

800

700

Nick's Chair

Blindhurst Fell

River Brock

Parlick

Blindhurst

△

THE BLEASDALE FELLS
CIRCULAR WALK.

Fell Foot

Scale

| ¼ | ½ | ¾ | 1 mile |

N

Car Parking

2

A WALK OVER THE BLEASDALE FELLS.
A CIRCULAR WALK OF 7½ MILES.

This is a fairly strenuous walk suitable for those readers with fellwalking experience, and a map, compass, boots and proper clothing are essential. Remember to allow sufficient time to complete the walk and choose a clear day because the views seen from Fair Snape Fell are spectacular.

The distinctive shapes of Parlick Pike, Blindhurst Fell and Fair Snape Fell dominate the skyline to the east of the Wyre District. The River Brock starts its journey westwards from the slopes of these fells to join the River Wyre near to the village of St. Michaels.

Our excursion takes us over these fells which are subject to Access Agreements negotiated between the landowners and the Lancashire County Council. The right of access to these areas is conditional and we, for our part, have to observe the requirements of the Access Byelaws. This means that <u>no</u> dogs can be taken on this walk and on no account can fires or stoves be lit. Readers must also be aware that access may be prohibited on certain days in the months of August, September and October when grouse shooting takes place and at other times of high fire risk.

Our walk starts at the road junction at the end of the lane to Fell Foot (Grid ref. 602442.) where there is informal roadside parking. Leaving the car we start up the lane, climbing steeply, to reach Fell Foot Farm, where the gate at the side takes us onto Parlick Pike. Do not go straight up the fell

following the clough but bear left up the path with a more gentle gradient around the western flank of the fell. After about 600yds we reach a wire fence coming down from the summit of Parlick Pike which we cross by means of a stile. Now our route goes alongside a ruinous drystone wall until we join a tractor track which we now must follow. We are now on Blindhurst Fell.

below us lies Bleasdale and in front of us is the long ridge leading up to the cairn, Paddy's Pole, on Fair Snape Fell. A quarter of a mile along the track brings us to a stile in a wire fence; here we turn left and follow the fence downhill until a dry-stone wall is reached (220yds). With the wall to our right we continue uphill to cross a wire fence by a stile (150yds). We are now on Fair Snape Fell. Some 330yds further on we arrive at Nick's Chair, a stony depression on the ridge, where a stone shelter has been constructed up against the wall. Continuing uphill the path runs

alongside the wall for about 200 yds then it veers away slightly to the west, its route being well-indicated by a series of stone cairns until Paddy's Pole is reached half a mile further on.

Although Paddy's Pole is not the true summit of the fell it is adorned with two cairns, a stone shelter and a triangulation point. The views from here are quite breathtaking. On a clear day you can see right across the Fylde Plain to the Irish Sea with the towns of Fleetwood, Blackpool and Southport, across the Ribble, evident. The Lakeland fells are visible to the north and sometimes, if you are lucky, you may be able to make out the Welsh Mountains and the Isle of Man.

The true summit lies about half a mile to the north east, it is marked with a cairn at the highest point of 1707 ft, close to the junction of two wire fences. To this cairn we must journey next over a rough terrain of peat hags resembling a lunar landscape. If the 1707' cairn cannot be seen, walk on a compass bearing of

58° from Paddy's Pole trig-point. From the 1707' cairn, after following the path through the peat hags for about 200 yds,

our route follows the fence northwards to Fiendsdale Head and the sign-board which marks the northerly corner of the Access Area. This mile long section

of the walk is a bit tedious and takes us across open moorland which is usually wet and boggy.

Things improve considerably after Fiendsdale Head when we cross the fence by means of a stile and head south-west along the path which goes

FAIR SNAPE AND PARLICK
FROM HOLME HOUSE FELL.

straight down the flank of Holme House Fell to join a wall near to a gate. We walk past the gate following the wall on our left which bends right and then left until we reach a gate through which we leave the fell. From the gate we walk straight ahead to join the track coming from Hazelhurst. We turn left here and follow it to Holme House where it passes behind the buildings.

Holme House was bequeathed to John Parkinson by his father Richard Parkinson of Hazelhurst in 1798.

HOLME HOUSE.

John married Margaret Rhodes and a stone over the front door records their initials and the date 1802. The word holme derives from the Old Norse "holmr" meaning island or water-meadow.

Crossing a stream, the River Brock, the track bears right and after approximately 215 yds. we leave it, turning sharp left and keeping a fence to our left, to reach a gate some 100 yds. from the track. Immediately through the gate we cross a culvert (take care here I nearly fell in) and walking straight ahead with the wall to our right we set off to Higher Fair Snape.

Higher Fair Snape comprises two 17th.-century farmsteads. The dwelling with the date-stone over the main entrance was once the home of the Parkinson family. The stone bears the family coat of arms, the initials R. P. (Ralph Parkinson) and the date 1637. The place is well-named...."fair snape" Old English meaning pleasant meadow. How very true!

To continue, the track takes us past farm buildings towards the farm houses where we turn right having a stone building to our

HIGHER FAIR SNAPE.

13

right. Walking past a water-trough we continue along the track in a south-westerly direction until we leave it turning left through a gate after walking some 100 yds. beyond the farm dwelling

We now proceed in front of Higher Fair Snape, keeping the fence to our left, towards a small wood. Before we get to the end of the path we go through a wooden gate on the left and into the small wood via a metal gate. Here we ford the stream and go through a wooden gate.

Bearing right we must now cross the fields aiming for a stile in a wire fence some 50 yds to the left of a large oak tree and at the foot of a track which can be seen climbing up the lowest shoulder of the fell. Within 120 yds of the stile we briefly join a farm track which fords a stream after which we veer

stile in fence

to the left to cross the stile. We now follow the track which climbs up the fell to the right to arrive at a gate in a fence.

Below is Blindhurst built by another member of the Parkinson family of Bleasdale, Richard Edward Parkinson. A date stone bears his initials and the date 1731.

We must ignore the gate and another track going up the fell and carry on walking alongside the hedge on our right. Through the gate at the Access signpost we walk straight ahead to the second signpost opposite which there is a stile in the wire fence. Over this stile we turn to our left to ford a stream just beyond a wire fence, no stile here, May 1990, but the fence is low enough to stride over. We

walk across the field, over another stream, to the middle of the wall opposite where we arrive at stone steps built into the dry-stone wall. Having climbed over the steps we head across the

field towards the left of a clump of trees in front of us. Over the stile we now walk towards the easterly end of Longridge Fell, crossing yet another stream, to a stile over a wall. From here the car parking area at the Fell Foot Lane junction comes into view and we can make our way to the starting point of the walk leaving the field through a gate at the corner.

A RIVERSIDE STROLL
AT ST. MICHEALS.

17

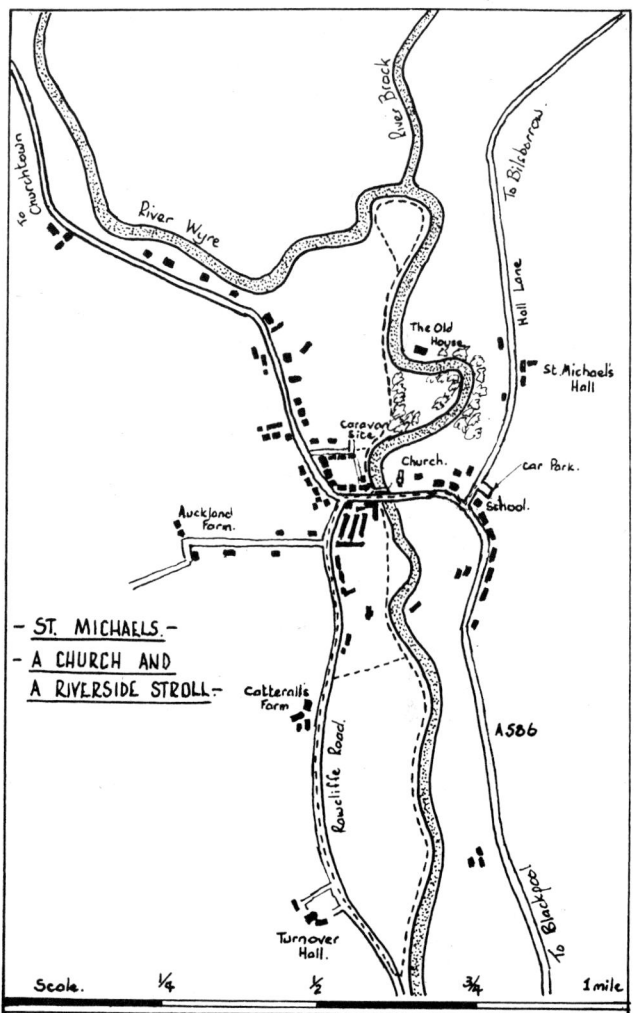

- ST. MICHAELS. -
- A CHURCH AND
A RIVERSIDE STROLL -

Scale.   ¼   ½   ¾   1 mile

18

ST. MICHAELS RIVER SIDE STROLL.
A TWO AND A HALF MILE WALK.

This walk is included for the benefit of a friend and fellow jazz musician who likes a very easy short walk, good scenery, a bit of local history and a village pub in close proximity. This excursion meets all his criteria.

Ample car parking is available at the Parish car park on Hall Lane. On leaving the car park we turn left to join the main road, A586, and then right to the old church that gave the village its name. It is well worth a visit.

The church, which is dedicated to St. Michael the Archangel, was listed in the Domesday Book, 1086, as MICHELESCHERCHE. It was built at a safe crossing of the river round about 650 AD. Nothing remains of the original building although the stone base of the sundial in the churchyard is thought to be the base of a Saxon cross. The present building has a long history.

1200. circ.	St Michaels church nove built or rebuilt.
1241.	Church becomes a vicarage.
1250.	Building enlarged.

1274 -1327.	The church mentioned in the Testa de Nevill.
1402.	Enlarged and re-roofed. King Henry IV giving four oak trees for this purpose.
1480.	Butler chapel founded by John Butler of Rawcliffe.
1500 circ.	South chancel aisle added.
1529.	Lady chapel added.
1540.	Two chantries closed.
1544.	Diocese of Chester finally defined and organised, St. Michaels church attached thereto.
1549 circ.	Tower built.
1570.	A vestry was added.
1608.	An impost levied by the Bishop of Chester showed that there was a vicarage at St. Michaels.
1611.	Restoration carried out by Henry Butler. His initials and arms together with the date 1611 can be seen on the parapet of the tower. This date can be seen over the doorway of the south porch.
1626.	Roof rebuilt.

1671. Clock installed.

1797. Butler chapel restored.

1811. Roof raised.

1850. Clock replaced.

1852. Restoration work carried out.

Allen Clarke in his book "More Windmill Land" states that in the churchyard there can be found the grave of a local artist who was called Barrow and born in Great Eccleston in 1737. He was a good friend of the famous artist George Romney, 1734-1802, who was born in Lancashire and who was noted for his portrait painting and for his admiration of Lord Nelson's Lady Hamilton. Inside the church, which contains many interesting historical features, a helpful guide book can be obtained for the sum of fifty pence.

Leaving the church we continue our walk by crossing the river over the footbridge and passing the "Grapes" we come to the village shop and post office on the corner of Rawcliffe Road. Here we turn left and walk up Rawcliffe Road for about 3/4 of a mile until on our left and just past Turnover

23

Hall we arrive at a sign post and stile on our left. Take care on this section of the walk as Rawcliffe Road is a fairly busy highway and a footpath exists for only part of the way. We climb the stile and head back towards the village on the river embankment built to alleviate the problems of flooding experienced in these parts. Soon the village and church come into view and we arrive at the bridge where we cross the busy main road with care to join a tarmacadam path directly opposite.

In this vicinity you may come across the ghost of Major Ralph Longworth a veteran of the Civil War and a former owner of Old St. Michaels Hall, demolished over 100 years ago. He had seen much action in the war and was promoted to the rank of Major in 1689 when he was in his sixties. Tradition has it that his ghost used to haunt the river bank, in the vicinity of the site of the old Hall so persistently, that a local priest had to confront the troubled spirit. It was laid to rest under the bridge with the command that he must be quiet never getting up any more either for his own recreation or to scare the fearful "so long as water ran downhill and ivy grew green".

Do not be deterred we must carry on walking for this is the most delightful part of our excursion. The tarmacadam path takes us alongside the river through trees to an open field where we walk along the flood embankment to where the River Brock joins the River Wyre. This is a spot well known to anglers so tarry a while and admire the scenery with the familiar profiles

27

of Harrisend Fell, Fairsnape Fell and Parlick Pike visible to the east on a clear day. From here we have to retrace our route back to the bridge where we turn left to make our way back to the car-park or perhaps right to the "Grapes" for refreshment.

A WALK TO LADY HAMILTON'S WELL.

LADY HAMILTON'S WELL.
A CIRCULAR WALK OF APPROXIMATELY FOUR
MILES FROM GARSTANG.

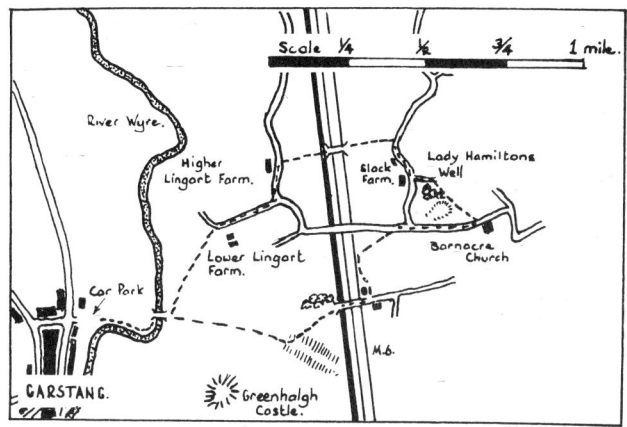

Our walk starts from the car park at the Community Centre, Garstang. At the time of writing alterations were taking place to this building to provide a Tourist Information and Discovery Centre. A visit may be worth our while as the intention is to highlight the flora, fauna and history of this attractive area.

Leaving the car park we walk upstream along the bank of the River Wyre around the edge of the sports field. At the concrete bridge we climb the steps turning right at the top to cross the river. Here are the giant sluice gates, controlled by huge hydraulic rams, which have been installed to control flooding, a major problem over many years further down the river.

We are now proceeding along the track bed of the former Garstang and Knott End Railway. This section of the line was opened on the 5th. December 1870 and was finally closed in 1963. A locomotive named "Farmers' Friend" was purchased in 1876, it's whistle was said by the locals to sound like a dying pig. Although it was sold in 1883 it operated long enough to give the railway the name by which it is remembered to this day, the "Pilling Pig".

Across the fields to our right can be seen the remains of Greenhalgh Castle built in 1490. It withstood a two year siege in support of the Royalist cause until it capitulated in 1645. By 1649 it lay in ruins, all that survives is the remains of one of the four corner towers.

Soon the embankments and cutting of the old railway are clearly recognizable and after negotiating 4 stiles we soon arrive at the cutting. Locals can still remember when Royal Trains were shunted here to allow the passengers a rest in secluded surroundings on their journeys to and from Scotland. The cutting is now a haven for wild life where you may catch a glimpse of foxes and where you will most certainly see many rabbits.

We do not walk down this corridor, instead we walk up the rising bank to our left to a stile which is at the end of a hawthorn hedge. Over the stile we head diagonally across the field past a single tree to the corner near the wood to arrive at a concrete ladder stile. Two bridges take us across the main line railway and the busy M.6. motorway towards a house with the date 1730 on the door lintol. We turn left before we reach the house and passing a barn on our left we enter a field where we head towards the fence which bounds the M.6.

This section of the M.6. was the first part of the motorway system, being opened in 1958. It is still noted for the attractive design of the many bridges which cross over it. The section some 14 miles long from junction 32 at Broughton to junction 33 just north of Forton, was designed by James Drake, County Surveyor and Bridgemaster.

At the end of the fence we climb over two stiles just a few yards apart and head towards the far right hand corner of the field walking alongside the hedge and fence at the edge of the stream. On reaching the stile, which we climb over onto the road, we turn right following the road uphill for some 600 yards to Barnacre Church.

This beautiful little church, dedicated to All Saints, was built by Thomas Henry Rushton, a textile magnate from East Lancashire, in 1905. His son, Thomas, is buried in the churchyard. He was a pilot during World War Two and lost his life when he was 29 years old.

Just before the church on the left there is a red post box and it is from here that

we go down some steps to cross a stream
over a wooden footbridge then turning left
we walk towards the fence line. Over the
stile we now walk diagonally across the field
to the brow of the hill where we walk past
the top of a disused quarry. This is a good
place to stop and rest with good views over
the Fylde plain and plenty of entertainment
provided by the large colony of rabbits
which inhabits the disused quarry below.
From here we go down the hill along the
side of a wood to go over a stile at the

bottom where we turn right to find Lady Hamilton's well bubbling among the bushes.

The Duke of Hamilton of Ashton Hall, now the Lancaster Golf Club, owned land in the district and his family intermarried with a local family, the Gerrards of Garstang. He lived several months of the year at Wedacre or Woodacre Hall not far from the well and it was from there that his Lady used to come to drink the medicinal waters. She may have even bathed as the well had steps down into the water. It is now overgrown and much of the stone work has collapsed but enough remains to give an idea as to its original shape. The water flows as readily as ever and, who knows, it may still possess its healing properties. Dean Swift described Lady Hamilton as being "handsome and airy with abundance of wit" and as having "a diabolical temper". It is reported that she, being a staunch upholder of both Church and State, took out her whip to drive the Garstang Independents out of their little chapel.

Leaving the well we cross the field

diagonally to a stile from where we climb the farm track to join the road, Keepers Lane. Here we turn right and walk down the road past Crosby Cottage to a stile on the left. Over the stile we must now walk alongside the hedge and then across the field heading for the footbridge which will take us back over the M.6. A stile takes us onto the footbridge then another leads us to a crossing over the main Euston to Glasgow railway line. Here, dear reader, we cross with caution taking great care to look out for approaching trains. From the crossing we go straight ahead through a field to a road, Hazelhead Lane, where we turn left. Where the road bends sharp left we leave it by going down the unmade farm track on the right. Where this track bends to the right we will locate a stile in the hedge on our left. We climb over this stile and head along a footpath over the fields and, after crossing three stiles, we arrive at the Pilling Pig track bed from where we retrace our steps back to the car park, our starting point.

A WALK IN AND AROUND
THE VILLAGE OF PILLING.

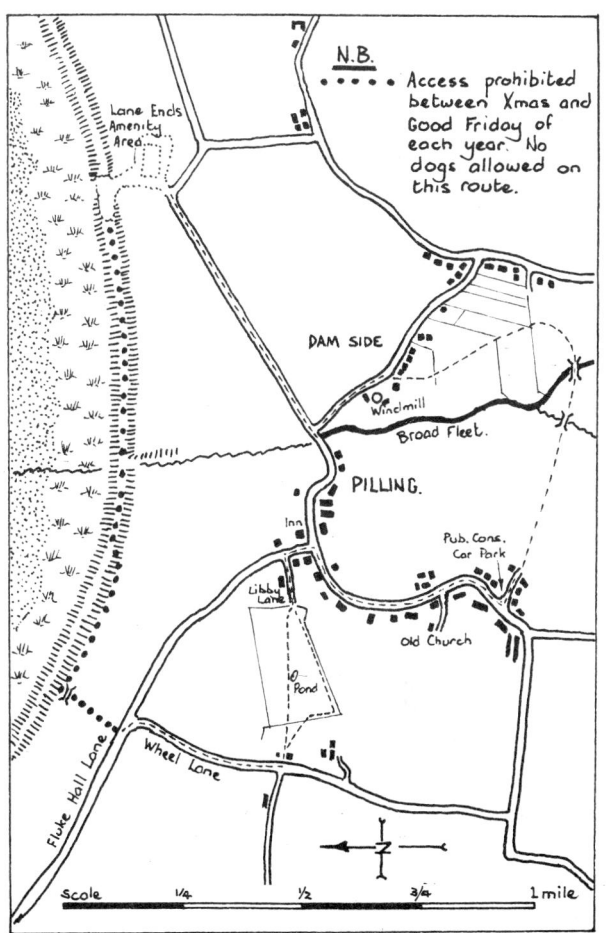

N.B.
•••••• Access prohibited between Xmas and Good Friday of each year. No dogs allowed on this route.

Lane Ends Amenity Area

DAM SIDE

Windmill

Broad Fleet.

PILLING.

Inn

Pub. Cons. Car Park

Libby Lane

Old Church

Pond

Fluke Hall Lane

Wheel Lane

N

Scale   ¼   ½   ¾   1 mile

A WALK IN AND AROUND THE VILLAGE OF PILLING.

Introduction   APPROX. FOUR MILES.

The countryside around Pilling bears no resemblance to how it looked some four and a half thousand years ago. Then the land was covered by a large forest. There is a theory that the forest was destroyed by a severe storm and flooding by the sea but it is more likely that climatic changes brought about its destruction when conditions became very wet. To this day farmers dig up the remains of this forest from their land. These remains are known locally as bog-oak.

Peat began to form at some time between the Neolithic Age and the Early or Middle Bronze Age. Stone artifacts have been found in the area in clay under the peat formation whilst bronze axes were found in the peat near to the bottom of the layer. The early settlers were cut off from the rest of the country by the sea and the inhospitable bog. An ancient walk-way called Kate's Pad enabled safe passage across the moss. It was constructed of timber and walking must have been very precarious for, when a section was excavated in 1950, it was revealed that one plank was only 8 inches wide. In 1744 Pilling Moss was observed to rise and then sink before moving southwards covering 20 acres of land in half an hour. It was drained in the 19th century and as a result the peat has consolidated. Over a hundred years ago it was said to have been 12 ft. deep, now the depth varies between 6 and 4 ft. There is an old saying:

> "Once a wood
> And then a sea
> Now a moss
> And aye will be."

There is no mention of Pilling in the Domesday Book, 1086, but it is recorded in a grant from Theobald Walter made between 1194 and 1199.

The name Pilling is derived from the Celtic " Pyll" meaning a creek and "ing" a diminutive.

The Walk.

Please note that this walk takes us across land owned by North West Water and access is prohibited from Christmas until Good

Friday. This is to protect over-wintering birds and also not to disturb sheep during the lambing season. Dogs are strictly prohibited.

Our walk starts at the car-park at the Lane Ends Amenity Area from where we proceed in a westerly direction over a stile and along the embankment built to protect the village from the sea. Over another stile at Broad Fleet our route is well waymarked and soon the markers lead us down from the top of the embankment to ground level where we proceed to a stile at a concrete bridge. Here we leave the embankment turning left to follow a track across the field to a stile which takes us onto Fluke Hall Lane. (During the "prohibited" period an alternative route can be used to arrive at this point). We turn left then right to go down Wheel Lane. At the first house on our left, Springfield Cottages, a stile and a waymarker indicates our way. From here there are two ways across the fields to Libby Lane, one ahead to another stile then diagonally across the field past a pond, the other around the field boundary. Down Libby Lane we reach a road where we turn right to arrive at another road junction.

At the road junction, with the school on our right and the Golden Ball to our left, we turn right and soon pass the Church of St. John the Baptist built in 1887. Just past the "Ship Inn" an unmade lane takes us to the "Old Church" which is well worth a visit.

The Old Church.

The original chapel serving Pilling was situated near Newers Wood and may have been in existence in Saxon times. It became too small to accommodate the local populace so it was demolished and a new church was built in 1717 and consecrated in 1721. It is now known as the "Old Church" and is a fine example of a Georgian church. Over the door there is a sundial inscribed "Thus Eternity approacheth — G. Holden 1766." George Holden was born in 1720 and was appointed to the Curacy of Pilling on the 11th May 1758 where he remained until September 1767. He was a famous mathematician and compiled the "Holden's Tide Tables" which are in use to this day. He died in 1793 and is buried at Bentham. The "Old Church" is no longer in

INTERIOR PILLING OLD CHURCH.

48

use but it is being maintained. It is kept locked to the public but arrangements can be made for parties to visit.

To continue with our walk we must retrace our steps back to the road along which we proceed to the car-park on the left hand side of the road. From here we turn left up the tarmacadam lane past the childrens' play area, through a wooden gate, to an old farmyard. With a building with a sign "EFFICIENTA" to our right we go through a metal gate and through the right hand metal gate of the two gates that face us. Down a short lane we go through a small gate into a field where we follow the fence line to our left to a small footbridge and stile over a ditch. From here we have to go straight ahead to a well-constructed footbridge where we cross the Broad Fleet. From the bridge we bear left and walk diagonally across the field to a kissing gate in a hedge from where we bear left and walk across the next field, in the general direction of the windmill, to another kissing gate in a hedge. Through the gate we proceed to stile and then on towards a white gate from where we carry on down a narrow path, between two hedges, to the road. We are now at Dam Side. We turn left up the road passing the windmill on our left.

The Windmill.

There have been mills in this location for many centuries. There is a mention of a water mill in a recorded dispute between the Abbot and Convent of Leicester and the Abbot and Convent of Cockersand in 1242. Dam Side owes its name to the dam which existed to supply the power to drive the water mill. Mentioned in a Deed of Division dated the 13th February 1764 was the presence of two mills, one worked by water and one by wind. This is confirmed by Yate's Map of 1786. A complaint was made to the owners of the water mill that on the 28th Sept. 1817 lands were flooded by the overflow of water from Pilling Water "occasioned by a weir across the same for the purpose of conveying water to a certain water corn mill called Pilling Mill." The present windmill was built by Ralph Slater in 1808. It was

completed in just three weeks and, with the original wooden cap, stood 73' tall. It had six storeys with a balcony, the reefing stage, encircling the mill at the second storey. The sails provided the power to turn four sets of unusually large stones, one being 6ft in diameter. There is a local legend which tells the story of a young farm worker who agreed to be tied to a sail as a bet to win a gallon of beer. He managed one revolution before shouting to be released having had enough of the experience. Whether or not he was awarded the prize is not known. The drying room was said to be the same as used by the former water mill. In 1886 the sails were removed when it was converted to steam. It ceased working in 1926 and was later converted into a dwelling house.

Our walk continues as we leave the windmill and arrive at Broad Fleet bridge. This structure replaced an earlier bridge and was built in two parts, the first being completed in 1783 and the second in 1840. The original course of the Broad Fleet

was through what is now the garden of the old Vicarage; a single straight channel now allows the flow of a greater volume of water.

Local legend has it that the Devil, Owd Nick, engaged in a battle of wits with a Cockerham schoolmaster in the 1700s. The schoolmaster set Owd Nick a task which he was unable to complete and come out the victor; it is very difficult to plait the fine Cockerham sand! In a rage Owd Nick leapt from Cockerham Church to land on Broad Fleet Bridge where his hoof was imprinted. His next leap took him into the River Wyre at Fleetwood and the third onto the Pennystone Rock at Bispham which split in two on impact.

Have a look for the hoof-mark on the parapet of the bridge. Try the left-hand side, facing Pilling, near to the garden of the Vicarage.

To complete our walk and return to the Lane Ends Amenity Area we turn right at Broad Fleet Bridge and follow the road.

SKIPPOOL AND LITTLE POULTON
CIRCULAR WALK.

A CIRCULAR WALK FROM SKIPPOOL TO LITTLE POULTON AND BACK. APPROX. THREE AND THREE QUARTER MILES.

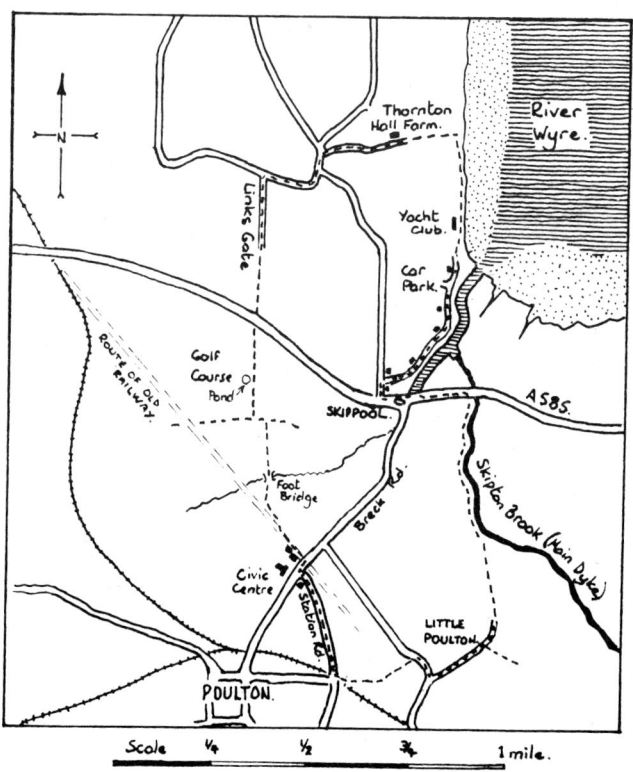

Our walk starts from the carpark at Skippool, thought to have got its name from the Saxon word for a small boat, "skiff". We leave the carpark and head towards the creek where we turn left along the road past

the River House Restaurant towards the Yacht Club which is built on the site of an old bone mill.

Silcock's Bone Mill was built in the 1870s and animal bones shipped there were landed at a jetty and then processed into bone meal. The business was transferred to bigger premises in Liverpool and the factory was demolished in 1947 the site being acquired by the Blackpool and Fleetwood Yacht Club. Local legend has it that the ghost of a Victorian workman is seen in this vicinity, be warned!!

400 yds past the Yacht Club we leave the riverside path and follow the sign to Little Thornton. Stop at the top of the hill and admire the view towards the river; shortly further on we arrive at Thornton Hall Farm. Thornton probably derives its name from the Old English tun, or enclosure, of thorns. The name Torentun is recorded in the Domesday survey.

During the reign of King John, Margaret Wynewick held two of the six carucates of Torentun (one carucate is estimated to be 100 acres) and her marriage was in the King's gift. In 1215 Boldewinus Blundus paid 20 marks to the King for permission to marry her and to obtain her estate. Later we learn that in 1221 Michael de Carleton paid a fine of 10 marks to Henry III for marrying Margaret without royal assent. In 1258 it is recorded that Margaret de Carleton still held her land in Thornton in her maiden name. The Testa de Nevil states that a Matilda de Thorneton held land to the annual value of 20 shillings and that her marriage also lay in the King's gift. Later about 1323 a moiety of Thornton was held by Lawrence the son of Robert de Thorneton, a member of the same family. In 1346 John, son of Lawrence, is recorded as holding one carucate of land in Thornton and Staynolfe. In 1421 John died and his half of the manor of Thornton passed to his son William who died aged 30yrs in 1429. The manor was held by Thomas Earl of Derby in 1521 and this passed into the hands of the Fleetwoods of Rossall. Sir Peter Hesketh Fleetwood founded the town of Fleetwood and bankrupted himself in the process and in 1875, after his death, his estate, manorial rights and privileges were purchased by the Fleetwood Estate Co. There is little information about the Thorntons of Thornton but it is thought that they resided in Thornton Hall near to the site of the present Thornton Hall Farm.

Our route takes us past the farm and

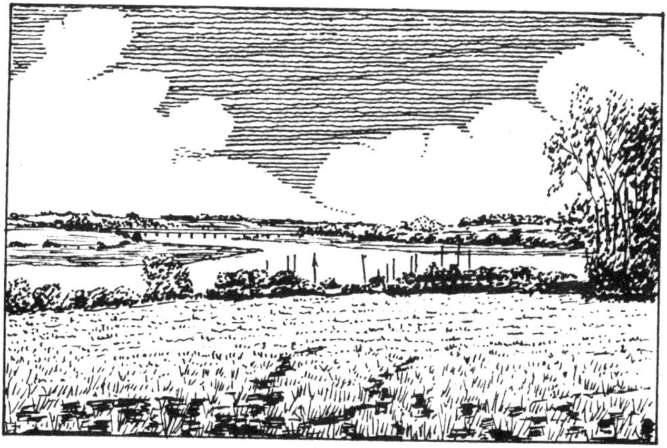

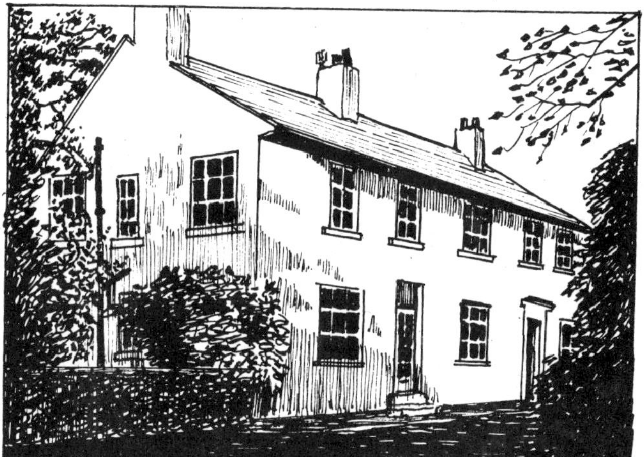

down Woodhouse Road to the main road which we cross and proceed down Tarn Road until Links Gate is reached. We turn left here to the top of a slight incline where we climb a stile and proceed across a field to the A 585, Amounderness Way. Please take care crossing this busy road. Now the walk continues across the golf course, a route which is usually well waymarked. A finger post points our way along a grooved path past a pond and keeping a hedge to our right we reach a waymarking post. Here our path crosses another public footpath from Rington to Skippool. From the waymarker we go ahead slightly to the left to follow a ditch and a hedge to a white footbridge over a stream. Over the bridge we turn right and head for a tall hedge which we follow to a stile. Over the stile we are now on the track bed of the old Preston and Wyre Railway along which we continue forward at the back of some buildings to arrive at Breck Road. From here we proceed down Station Road at the side of the Royal Oak.

Here once stood Poulton's first railway

station opened in July 1840 and the Railway and Station Hotel stood on the land now occupied by the car showrooms. At about this time an old dyehouse was demolished and the Royal Oak Hotel was later built on the site. A brook which had long been polluted by effluent from the dyehouse was culverted; this was the brook over which the town's cuckstool or ducking stool had operated. This was once the scene of a tragic accident. On the 1st July 1893 the 11 o'clock holiday special from Blackpool approached the curve leading into the station, the brakes failed and the train left the track. There were many casualties and three lives were lost including that of the driver, Cornelius Ridgway. It was to the Railway and Station Hotel that the bodies and casualties were taken. Three years later the present railway station was opened at the top of Breck Road with safer approach curves from Blackpool.

Continuing our walk we go some 500 yds. down Station Road to the railway bridge where we take a path to our left which leads to Howarth Crescent. At the

end of Howarth Crescent a footbridge takes us over the old partially filled railway cutting and then onto to Moorland Road where we turn right past the school and then left into Little Poulton Lane.

Little Poulton was once a hamlet separate from the town of Poulton but in modern times it has been enveloped by the growth of the town. It is now a pleasant mixture of old and new superior dwellings. The present Little Poulton Hall stands on land close to where the original mansion once stood. In 1570 it was occupied by George Hesketh who married

Dorothy Westby of Mowbreck. Their son, William, married Elizabeth Allen of Rossall Hall and they had two children, William and Wilfred. William, the eldest, seems to have gone to live at Mains Hall. Little Poulton descended in the Heskeths of Mains Hall but the family name changed after a marriage with the Brockholes family of Claughton to Hesketh-Brockholes. About 1750 the estate passed to William Fitzherbert who also assumed the name of Brockholes. It is recorded that in 1839 Thomas Fitzherbert - Brockholes farmed 814 acres of land at Little Poulton.

Walking down the lane it is easy to imagine what the hamlet once looked like. At the end of the lane just past Little Poulton Hall we climb a stile and keeping the hedge to our right walk to another stile. From here following a waymarking arrow we cross a field to arrive at Main Dyke formerly Skipton Brook.

This watercourse flows from Marton Mere to discharge into the River Wyre at Skippool; it is important in providing drainage to an extensive area of land in the Fylde.

We follow the stream to another stile from where our way goes through a wooded area and, passing the rear of houses and a caravan park on our left, we emerge at the A585. Crossing with care we turn left passing the imposing River Wyre Hotel which bears the Brockholes coat of arms to arrive at the roundabout where we turn right into Skippool Road. After a few yards we turn right into Wyre Road and pass the Thornton Lodge Hotel.

Here at Skippool try and imagine the scene when this was once a busy port.

66

At one time it is said that the trade at Wardleys and Skippool exceeded that at the Port of Liverpool, there were reports of press-gangs, smuggling and cock-fighting at Skippool. A popular alehouse, the Ouzel Inn, stood on land adjacent to where the Thornton Lodge Hotel stands some 200yrs. ago. In 1627 Dorothy Shaw wife of Thomas, "joyner of Skippoole" was accused by a neighbour, William Wilkinson, of being a witch. He called her a "witch and demdyke" and said "thou art a witch God bless me ...... I am affrayed for my wife, children and goods."

Returning to the peace and tranquillity of modern Skippool we follow the road passing the dwelling house Tarn Hows, which was built around 1741 as a warehouse, to the carpark to complete our walk.

A WALK IN AND AROUND
GREAT ECCLESTON.

A WALK IN AND AROUND GREAT ECCLESTON OF APPROXIMATELY FOUR MILES.

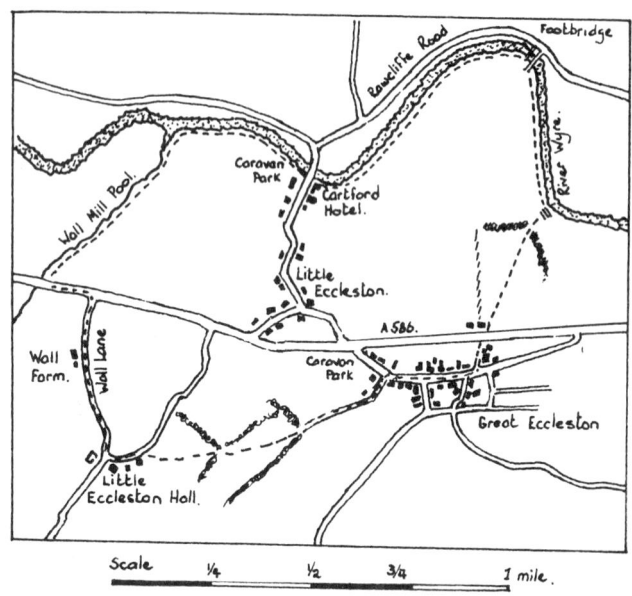

Our walk starts at the Market Square in the centre of the village of Great Eccleston. Here we park the car and proceed up the High Street in the direction of Garstang. After approximatley 150 yds we arrive at a signpost on our left indicating

a bridleway. Here we turn left and immediately leave the bridleway following a public footpath signpost which directs us between a brick building on our right and a green painted garage on the left. We soon arrive at the main road, the A586, which we cross with care and then climb the stile at the side of a gate directly in front of us. Here a sign post points the way diagonally across the field to a gate, at the side of which is another stile. Over this stile and walking alongside the hedge to our right we climb the concrete steps onto the flood embankment of the River Wyre. Turning to our left and heading downstream route finding could not be any easier, we just have to follow the course of the river. Approximately 800 yds. along the embankment we pass a footbridge and an aqueduct crossing the river and soon the houses at Cartford Lane come into view. Rounding a bend in the river the Cartford Bridge can now be seen; here we leave the embankment and following a track past

the side of the Cartford Hotel to arrive at Cartford Bridge.

Before the bridge was built in 1831 the river could be crossed here by fording it at low water or by boat. The Squire of Out Rawcliffe, Thomas Robert Wilson-Ffrance, built the bridge; the fact that his wife, Mary, was terrified of crossing the river probably influenced this decision. Two girls, one a servant at the Hall, fell into the water when crossing by boat and narrowly escaped drowning and Mrs. Ffrance on hearing the news declared that she would not cross the river again until the bridge was built. The bridge is one of two over the River Wyre where a toll has to be paid to cross over it.

Continuing our walk we cross the road, Cartford Lane and, going over a stile, rejoin the river embankment. With the caravan park on our left we follow the river's curve until after approximately 550 yds we arrive at a watercourse, Wall Mill Pool, where it flows into the river. Turning sharp left we now walk

towards the A586 along the flood embankment of the stream. A stile takes us onto this road where we turn left and, after a few yards, cross it with caution to go down Wall Lane.

Soon we pass Wall Farm, a very old building with material dating from the 16th century. Note the number of bricked up windows on the south gable.

Further along the lane we arrive at Little Eccleston Hall. Datestones at the rear of the house have the dates 1638 and 1671, the latter probably indicates when the original building was extended. The house

once belonged to the Ffrance family who
in 1828 succeeded to the Rawcliffe
estate and became squires at Rawcliffe over
the river. They undertook major drainage
work of the mosslands and transformed
them into rich agricultural land.

Ignoring the lane which leads off to our
right we walk past the front of the Hall
then round a bend to arrive at an old
interesting barn. Just beyond the barn
there is a gate with a stile alongside
on our right. Here we climb over the
stile and head diagonally across the
field to a gate at the corner of the

field. Through the gate we continue in the same direction across the next field heading for a stile in the hedge corner. Over the stile go straight ahead and a series of stiles takes us along a green lane to join the road where we turn right and head back to the Market Square and our car to complete the excursion.

A WALK IN AND AROUND THE VILLAGE OF CHURCHTOWN.

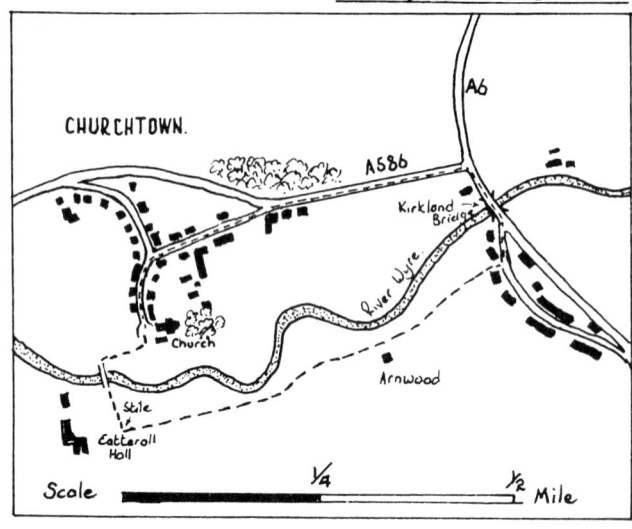

This short and easy walk gives one the
opportunity of visiting the lovely village of
Churchtown and the beautiful old church
dedicated to St. Helen which has rightly
been described as the "Cathedral of the
Fylde". Our walk starts from the car park
at the side of the church. Please note
that this car-parking area belongs to the
church and, whilst there are no objections

to its use by visitors, it must be kept clear on Sundays for the exclusive use of worshippers at the church. From here, at the rear of the church, a path takes us along a flood embankment to a modern pedestrian suspension bridge over the River Wyre.

A word of warning...... in and around these parts, according to Allen Clarke in his book "More Windmill Land", there exists a giant boggart with the intriguing name of Crappencrop. It is usually seen in the evening twilight and it has been known to startle horses and cause cyclists to fall of their bicycles. It is supposed to live under a boulder stone which is said to revolve when the church bells ring.

To proceed we cross the bridge and continue straight ahead to the field corner where there is a wooden stile on our left. On our right is Catterall Hall, a mid 18th-century building. We climb the stile to a good raised track which takes us across

the field and then over a cattle grid. At
a sharp bend in the river we go through
a white gate and over a cattle grid and,
passing a house on our right,'Arnwood;'
Kirkland Bridge comes into view. This
stone bridge carries the busy A.6.
road over the River Wyre.

   Allen Clarke tells of the existence
of a large watermill on the south side
of the river between Churchtown and the
bridge which was said to be destroyed
by fire in 1858. Yates map of 1786
however does not indicate a mill

KIRKLAND BRIDGE

84

in this location and there do not appear to be any obvious remains of such a building.

Our route takes us to a gate at the end of the track, through the gate we turn left onto a road which joins the A.6. Over the bridge we turn left up the A.586 road which will take us back to Churchtown. Here there is a fine avenue of trees and to our right, not always visible from the road through the trees, is Kirkland Hall which was built in 1760 for the Butler family. Passing the Horns Inn we leave the main road and follow the road which takes us to the 18th century village market cross; note the sundial on the south face. In times, not so long ago, markets and pot fairs were held at this location. From here we turn left and, passing the Punchbowl Inn and the neighbouring Churchgate House, 1698, we arrive back at the church to the start of our walk. Before we leave Churchtown a visit to St. Helen's Church

ST. HELEN'S CHURCH.

86

is strongly recommended.

St. Helen's the Cathedral of the Fylde.

St. Helens is the ancient Parish Church of Garstang and was built before the town of Garstang developed. On fairly recent maps the settlement around the church was shown as Garstang Churchtown. The precise age of the church is not known, the earliest reference to its existence being made in a document dated 1190. Until 1746 the circular churchyard was surrounded by two branches of the river and it is thought that it may have been a sacred site in pre-Christian times.

1180. circ.	The church was enlarged by the building of the north aisle, the original pillars remain.
1215.	The Abbey of Cockersand at Cockerham obtains the right to appoint the vicar of Garstang, this continued up to 1539.
1250. circ.	The south aisle was added.
1300.	West window south of tower built, present glass Victorian.
1320.	West window north of tower

built, present glass Victorian

1349. 2,000 persons died of the Black Death in the Parish.

1402. Henry IV gave four oak trees "for the reparation of Garstang Church".

1450. The church tower was built.

1499. A chantry chapel at the east end of the south aisle was endowed by Roger de Brockholes.

1529. The lady chapel was endowed by Margaret Rigmayden of Wedacre.

1570. The vicar's vestry was built. It is built of different stone than the rest of the church and, because it is badly fitted onto the church, it is thought to have been bought from Cockersand Abbey.

1632. So many parishioners died of the Plague that entries in the burial register ceased. A grave stone near to the vestry marks the resting place of Elizabeth Foster who died of the Plague.

1646. The pulpit was built.

1715. Local men who took part in

the 1715 Rebellion were hanged in Garstang. The graveyard at St. Helen's is the final resting place for three of them; Thomas Cartmell, Joseph Goose and Joseph Wadsworth.

1746. The River Wyre flooded the village and it was thought that the foundations of the church were so damaged as to require the demolition and rebuilding of the church on a safer site. The man hired to do the work found the foundations to be sound so, instead, he carried out repairs and dug a new bed for the river to divert it away from the church. The brass chandelier in the nave was presented to the church by this man from the profit he made out of this undertaking.

1757. Sundial installed in the churchyard
1811. Roof rebuilt and raised.
1823. Church gates provided.
1868. Restoration of the interior

carried out and the church rededicated by the Bishop of Tennessee who was attending the first Lambeth conference.

1990.   Celebrations marking 800 years at St. Helen's.

A WALK IN BLEASDALE

A WALK IN BLEASDALE.

A CIRCULAR WALK OF APPROX. FIVE AND A HALF MILES.

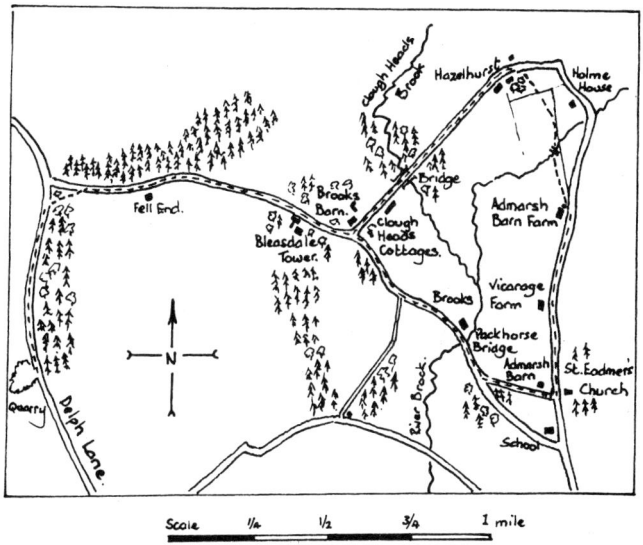

The biggest problem for the walker in the Bleasdale area is car parking. The roads are narrow and the road verges soft and no cars are allowed on the Bleasdale private estate. With all these problems in mind this walk starts from and finishes at the old quarry on Delph Lane where there is off-road parking for several cars. The grid reference is 546455.

From here we head northwards along Delph Lane for just over half a mile where there is a gap in the drystone wall on our left and a notice on a tree which says "No Cyclists". We go through the gap and follow a short path through the trees to a wooden gate and then on to the estate road where we turn right. We now must follow this road through a gate at Fell End to Bleasdale Tower. Here a notice warns us to go slowly "Horses and Children Everywhere".

We pass Bleasdale Tower to arrive at Brooks Barn where we take the road to our left past the farm then past the Clough Heads Cottages to the stone bridge over Clough Heads Brook.

The Bleasdale Estate was sold by Robert Parkinson Jnr. to William Garnett in 1842. He built Bleasdale Tower and, in 1857, established the North Lancashire Reformatory School. Clough Heads Cottages housed the boys who spent three years in residence learning to be better citizens, and working on the estate in order to acquire new skills for their future employment. The stone bridge over the brook was built by them, under supervision, and on the arch can be seen a carved tablet depicting the tools used in the construction of this their showpiece.

Half a mile along the road beyond the bridge we arrive at Hazelhurst.

Here at Hazelhurst there once stood a hamlet known Coolam; wool combing and straw hat manufacturing were the inhabitants' principal trades. It stood on an old drovers road which ran from Garstang to Dunsop Bridge and the packhorse bridge at Brooks was built on its route. Wool was transported as far as Halifax and Burnley. All that remains of the hamlet is a ruinous cottage but if you look closely at the field walls remains of mullioned windows, corner stones and door heads from other buildings in the hamlet can be seen.

Just after a clump of trees on our right we turn right and leave the track, avoiding the marshy area, to head diagonally to the left to a foot stile alongside a small wooden gate in a fence. Carrying on across the field we aim towards a metal gate with a stile alongside, over this we then cross the River Brock by means of two good foot-bridges or by fording. This is a pleasant spot at which to rest and admire the splendid scenery. To continue the walk we go along the track to Admarsh Barn Farm.

Avoiding the track which branches off to the right down to the farm we go straight ahead keeping close to the fence on our left and go behind a modern farm building through a narrow gap between this building and the fence to our left. Joining the estate road we turn right and soon pass Vicarage Farm on our right. Opposite the farm to our left and hidden in a clump of trees is the Bleasdale Circle.

This is an early Bronze Age burial mound dating from about 1800 B.C. The site comprised of a small mound 3ft. high and some 36ft across surrounded by a ring of eleven posts of oak, now marked by concrete pillars, with a ditch around them. In the centre of the mound a grave was found which contained two cremation urns both filled with charcoal and human bones. One of the urns held an incense cup. Around the mound was an outer circle of posts with a diameter of 150ft. This pallisade consisted of 22 large oak posts with smaller posts between them; this part of the site can not be seen. The inner burial mound was

not in the centre of the outer circle but almost touched it at the east. Please note that the Bleasdale Circle is on private land and permission to visit it has to be obtained at Vicarage Farm.

Leaving the farm we soon arrive at St. Eadmer's Church. The place of worship which has stood on this site for many years was once known as Admarsh Chapel, being re-named St. Eadmer when it was re-built in 1835. St. Eadmer was a friend of St. Anselm, Archbishop of Canterbury, during the reign of William Rufus. Windows from the Elizabethan Chapel can be seen built into the stonework of the tower.

Opposite the church on our right is Admarsh Barn with a date-stone over the door bearing the initials of Robert Parkinson and the date 1720. We take the

102

track in front of the barn through the gates which joins the estate road at a plantation. We turn right and go down to the road to pass Brooks on our right; here, spanning the River Brock, can be seen the old packhorse bridge. We soon arrive at the road junction at Brooks Barn where we bear left and then retrace our steps past Bleasdale Tower along the estate road to the path through the trees and back to Delph Lane. A left turn here takes us along the lane to the quarry and our car to complete our walk in Bleasdale.

A WALK THROUGH THE SALT WORKINGS OF PREESALL.

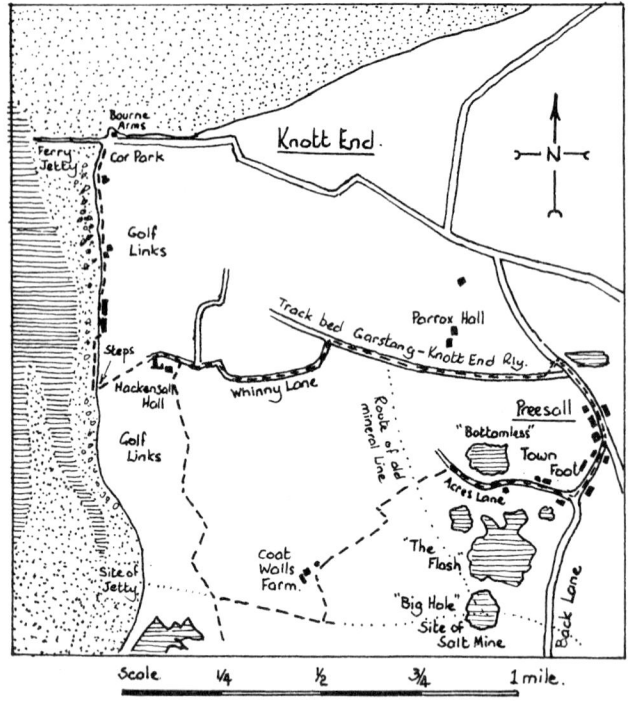

The Story of the Salt Industry in Preesall.

It was during the Triassic period some 200 million years ago when the salt deposits were laid as the result of a vast inland sea drying up. This was discovered in 1872 when, during a search for hematite, bore-holes were sunk and the salt deposit was found. In 1875 two local men sunk an 8ft. diameter well to the rocksalt and brine collecting at the bottom was pumped out. This enterprise was purchased by the Fleetwood Salt Co. in 1883, this company was taken over by the United Alkali Co. in 1890 which, in turn, was bought out by the Imperial Chemical Industry in 1926. Brine, an essential ingredient in chemical production, was pumped across the river to the factory at Thornton.

In addition to brine extraction a decision was taken to dry mine the rocksalt and mining commenced in 1893 when two shafts 20 yds. apart were sunk to depths of 470ft. and 900ft. The shafts were lined to make them watertight. The method of mining was to leave a roofing some 6ft thick supported by pillars of rocksalt 60ft. square and 105ft. apart. Salt was removed by under-cutting in lengths of 105ft. the distance between each pillar.

The mined rocksalt was taken by

mineral railway to a jetty near Arm Hill to be transported by boat to Widnes. Cargoes were also taken to the Continent, Australia and South America.

Steamer "Hermann" loading at Preesall jetty.

In 1912 a 1½ mile long mineral line was built to link the mine to the Knott End - Garstang Railway.

Bed of mineral line looking towards the jetty.

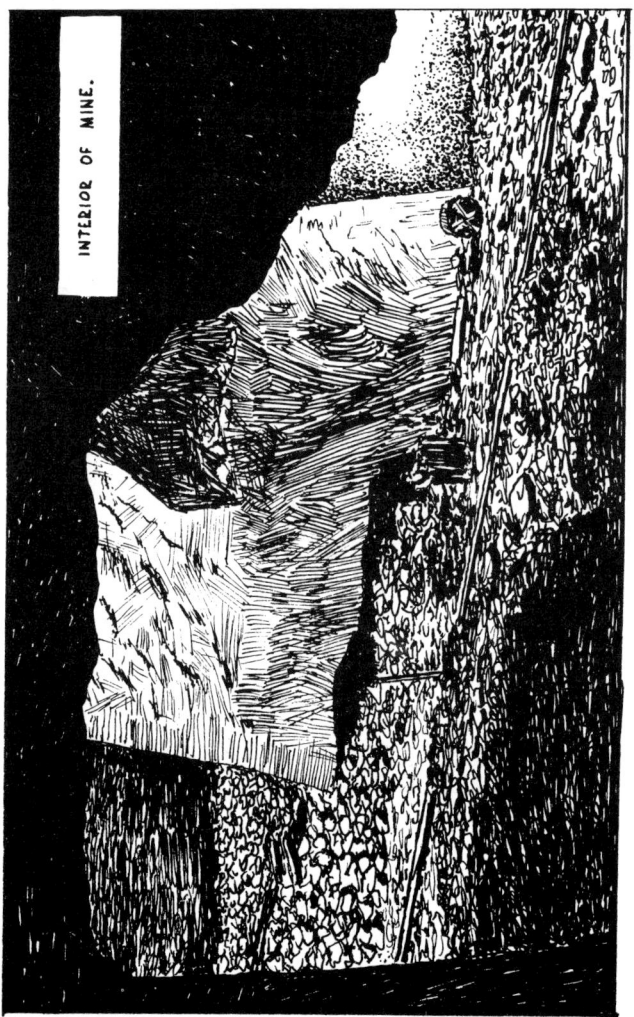

INTERIOR OF MINE.

108

Early methods of brine extraction led to land subsidence as the overlying marl roofs to the resultant cavities collapsed. In November 1901 an alarming incident occurred in an area known as North Field in which well nos 28, 29 and 30 had been sunk. Brine was first noticed penetrating into the mine in 1919 and in spite of remedial work over many years the problem persisted.

In June 1923 a depression was noticed at well 54 adjacent to Westfield Farm on Acres Lane. A hole appeared and by August it was 60 yds. in diameter and some of the farm buildings had to be pulled down. In November the former sold up and it was not until the next year that the crater was thought to have stabilised. Acres Lane was diverted and the farm demolished; the pit is known locally as "BOTTOMLESS".

The end of the mining operation started in June 1930 when water poured into the Upper Mine with " a roar which reverberated through the subterranean caverns"(Fleetwood Chronicle 6th June 1930). The miners were immediately evacuated. The cause was a

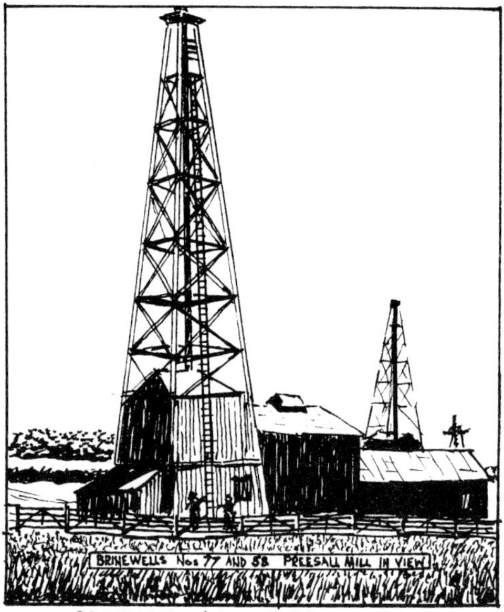

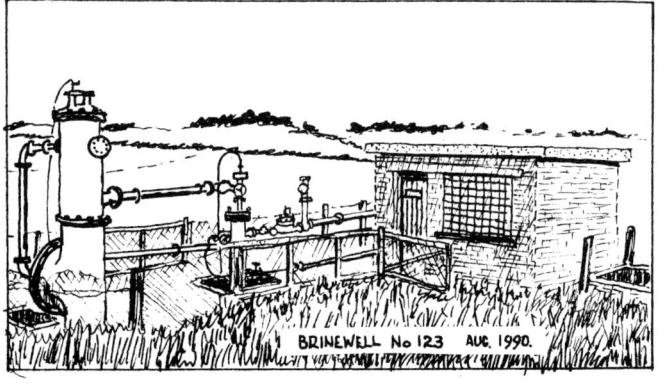

BRINEWELLS Nos 77 AND 58 PRESALL MILL IN VIEW.

BRINEWELLS ANCIENT AND MODERN.

BRINEWELL No 123   AUG. 1990.

subsidence on the surface at Clods Carr Lane which resulted in water penetrating the Upper Mine; the hole is known as the "FLASH." Clods Carr Lane provided access to Coat Walls Farm so a new road had to be made from Acres Lane. The pillars supporting the mine roof began to dissolve so the mine finally closed down in 1931 with brine being taken from it until 1934. This ceased when land adjacent to the shafts subsided to create the "BIG HOLE".

Today the pumping of brine across the river to the I.C.I chemical works continues as it forms the basis for the production of Chlorine in order to make poly-vinyl-chloride, P.V.C.

I.C.I. THORNTON.

There is plenty of salt left and quite recently new wells have been sunk. Modern technology ensures that no subsidence occurs and regular monitoring of surface levels is carried out.

One cannot help but wonder what the countryside would now look like had hematite been discovered in 1872 and not rocksalt.

<u>The Walk</u>.

Our walk starts at the car park behind the café adjacent to the ferry slipway. The café is located within the building which was once the Knott End Station on the Knott End to Garstang Railway.

Walking along the riverside promenade we pass in front of Sea Dyke Cottage to the cottages at Spring Bank. Here, in days long ago, customs officers would keep a look out for ships coming up the Wyre to the port of Wardleys. At the end of the promenade we descend the concrete steps to the shingle and carry on straight ahead until some wooden steps are reached. Up the steps and then along a

grooved path, Hackensall Hall is reached. Built in 1656 by Richard and Anne Fleetwood it replaced their residence at Rossall which had been damaged by the sea. Past the rear of the buildings we turn first right over a cattle grid to a track which we must now follow. After half a mile we arrive at the track bed of the mineral railway which ran from the Saltmine to Preesall Jetty. Ahead of us is the Barnaby's Sand Nature Reserve where the ungrazed saltmarsh creates a paradise for botanists and birdwatchers, but here we must turn left and head inland along the route of the railway line towards Coat Walls Farm.

Just past the farm we follow the track to our left which takes us past the side of the farm buildings. Soon a stile by a cattle grid is reached as the track takes us through the fields. Further on the path crosses the route of the mineral line which connected the Saltmine to the Knott End - Garstang Railway; its line can be traced across the fields. On a small hill to our right the ruined remains of the minehead building can be seen. Arriving at Acres Lane we climb the stile and turn right. The lane takes us between "Bottomless" on our left and the "Flash" on our right to Back Lane at Town Foot; here we turn left up the hill to the main road through Preesall Village where we turn left.

Here refreshments can be taken; the village has two inns, the Black Bull and The Saracen's

Head, and the establisments stand virtually side by side. The inn sign for the latter was so heavy that it caused the front wall to bulge and it had to be removed. "Owd Bigheyd" weighs 3 cwts and can be examined at close quarters in the

inn carpark.

Before we leave the village observe the round-shaped building on the right. In the 18th century Turnpike Trusts were established which enabled the cost of providing and maintaining roads to be met by the payment of tolls by the users. Funerals and local carts were exempt. This building was once a toll house in which the collector or pikeman worked and lived.

Leaving the village we follow the road down the hill and, just over the old railway bridge, we take a path to our left which takes us down to the bed of the former Knott End to Garstang railway branch line. This we follow until Whinny Lane is reached, where we leave the railway and follow the lane to Hackensall Hall. From here we retrace our steps along the riverside back to the carpark to complete our walk through the salt workings of Preesall.

READER'S PERSONAL LOG

WALK	DATE	NOTES	WEATHER	START	FINISH

WALK	DATE	NOTES	WEATHER	START	FINISH